Birthmark

Crab Orchard Award Series in Poetry

Birthmark

Jon Pineda

Crab Orchard Review

&

Southern Illinois University Press

Carbondale

Printed in the United States of America

07   06   05   4   3   2

The Crab Orchard Award Series in Poetry is a joint publishing venture of
Southern Illinois University Press and *Crab Orchard Review*. This series has been
made possible by the generous support of the Office of the President of Southern
Illinois University and the Office of the Vice Chancellor for Academic Affairs and
Provost at Southern Illinois University Carbondale.

Crab Orchard Award Series in Poetry Editor: Jon Tribble
Judge for 2003: Ralph Burns

Library of Congress Cataloging-in-Publication Data

Pineda, Jon, 1971–
   Birthmark / Jon Pineda.
     p. cm. — (Crab Orchard award series in poetry)
   I. Title. II. Series.
PS3616.I565 B57 2004
811'.6—dc22
ISBN 0-8093-2570-5 (pbk. : alk. paper)   2003017075

Printed on recycled paper. ♻

The paper used in this publication meets the minimum requirements of
American National Standard for Information Sciences—Permanence of Paper
for Printed Library Materials, ANSI Z39.48-1992. ⊗

For my mother and father.

For Ericka, always.

I don't blame you, I know

The place where you lie.

I admit everything. But look at me.

How can I live without you?

Come up to me, love,

Out of the river, or I will

Come down to you.

—*James Wright*

Contents

4. Undoing

Acknowledgments

Grateful acknowledgment is made to the editors of the following magazines where these poems first appeared:

Asian Pacific American Journal—"Between Rounds" and "Memory in the Shape of a House Made of Doors"
BigCityLit.Com—"Hunger"
Hayden's Ferry Review—"Corolla"
The Literary Review—"Matamis" and "Shelter"
Many Mountains Moving—"Willoughby Spit" and "Weight"
Pearl—"In Strange Circles"
Poetry Northwest—"Arboretum"
Puerto del Sol—"Five about Flowers" and "Living Together"
64 Magazine—"This Poetry"
To Topio—"A Shadow of Gulls"

"Wrestling" appeared in *Tilting the Continent: Southeast Asian American Writing*, edited by Shirley Geok-lin Lim and Cheng Lok Chua (New Rivers Press, 2000).

"A Few Words on Rome, *or* The Neighbor Who Never Waves" appeared in the anthology *Screaming Monkeys*, edited by M. Evelina Galang and Eileen Tabios (Coffee House Press, 2003).

"Birthmark," "Shelter," "Translation," and "This Poetry" appeared in the anthology *Asian American Poetry: The Next Generation*, edited by Victoria Chang (University of Illinois Press, 2003).

"Corolla" received a 1997 AWP *Intro* Award for poetry.

"In the Romance of Grief" is for Larry Levis.

I am especially grateful to the Virginia Commission for the Arts for a fellowship that enabled me to finish this manuscript.

My deepest gratitude to my family and my friends for their love and support.

To Nick Montemarano, John Moore, and Bill Tester for keeping the faith.

To Nick Carbó, Dave McCormack, and Oliver de la Paz for their invaluable guidance and generous friendship.

Deborah Digges, Greg Donovan, Robin Dunn, M. Evelina Galang, Linda Girardi, Eugene Gloria, Marita Golden, Vince Gotera, Lola Haskins, Terry Hummer, Luisa Igloria, Richard Katrovas, Yusef Komunyakaa, Laurie Kutchins, Bino Realuyo, Sheri Reynolds, Kim Roberts, Gary Sange, Tim Seibles, Leslie Shiel, Gerald Stern, Rivka Swensen, Philip Tabakow, Eileen Tabios, Amy Tudor, Ellen Bryant Voigt, and Alfred Yuson: friends and teachers whose encouragement helped shape this work.

Many, many thanks to Ralph Burns, Allison Joseph, Jon Tribble, and Southern Illinois University Press.

And, of course, for Amy, who always knew.

1

Half

It's what always begins

In half dark, in half light.

—*José Garcia Villa*

Matamis

One summer in Pensacola,
I held an orange this way,
flesh hiding beneath
the texture of the rind,
then slipped my thumbs
into its core & folded it
open, like a book.

When I held out the halves,
the juice seemed to trace
the veins in my arms
as it dripped down to my elbows
& darkened spots of sand.
We were sitting on the beach then,
the sun, spheres of light within each piece.
I remember thinking, in Tagalog,
the word *matamis* is sweet in English,
though I did not say it for fear
of mispronouncing the language.

Instead, I finished the fruit & offered
nothing except my silence, & my father,
who pried apart another piece, breaking
the globe in two, offered me half.
Meaning everything.

Wrestling

Before the season, we were already pissed,
our bodies tightening around ribs, our eyes,
like panthers, sinking into shadows.

We had given up food, sweat until
the air around us was heavy. The only thing
we cared about was winning.

At our first match, I wrestled a guy
I had met summers ago at a Filipino gathering,
some first communion or baptism.

By a man-made lake separating the neighborhood
in two, where most of the children had wandered,
a few of the boys pinned my shoulders against a tree

while one punched me. I could say it was because
I was only *half,* a mestizo, but that would be too easy.
We were just boys, happy in our anger.

When they let me go, their eyes clouded as the lake,
I didn't say a word. Years later, when I pulled
the one who had punched me down on the mat,

I watched the clock as I locked a breath inside his throat.
He could have been my brother, his hair the same
coarse black strands, his face filled with my shadow.

I held him there in front of everyone.

Memory in the Shape of a Swimming Lesson

If anything, it is like water.
Taking the shape of what surrounds it.
A concrete pool. The walls of a throat.
My earliest memory is of my father
standing at the edge, waving to me,
the tops of his hands more brown
from the summer, patting the water
now, & it is only in looking back,
I see he is doing what he thinks is right.
I am the first son, American-born.

It might even be a ritual, a father
taking his five-year-old into his arms
while children from other
Navy families run along the deck.
Lifeguards blow whistles, stop them
dead in their tracks.

Lifting him over the water,
the father offers his son up to fear.

The boy understands the word *mestizo*. It means "half-breed,"
not *full* Filipino. It is the word they use at parties
& touch his hair. They speak to him in Tagalog. He knows

it is the language his father speaks on the phone, or under his breath
when he is angry. The boy answers his father's questions in this language,
& some of the older Filipinos, those from an earlier generation, seem pleased.

It will mark his life. Years later, when the father leaves the family,
the boy forgets these words. They become, like the edge of the pool,
something he struggles to reach.

He crouches by the pool. He is saying, "Like this," & spooling his fingers together in the water. He is saying, his accent *broken* & unmistakably foreign, not to give up. There are only so many words he uses, some in English & some in Tagalog, & the boy, flailing his arms to stay afloat, understands none of them.

If anything, it is like learning to swim. Thrashing in the deep end,
the boy feels as if the water itself is a hand. He is sinking into its palm.
Though consumed with fear & the chill rising from the bottom,
he can see his father waving him toward the edge. As if he only needs
to make it there, & it will all be over.

Visitation, *or* How a Son Came to Resemble the Archangel

The children dig, dulling new plastic tools,
their backs to the surf never ceasing
to surprise them. The father watches
from a chair with only a few days left in it,

the woven nylon having ripped almost
everywhere but those few strands
that must hold it all together. So
much like the moment when he returns,

out of breath. With their shoes & shirts
scattered on the edge of the blanket, he knows,
Even in their excitement, there is abandon.
His oldest tilts a bucket of sand over a moat

filling with water. What they worked on
this day is falling apart. The walls slide
down, the turrets they made with dripping
sand begin to buckle, melting into the surf.

They scream as they work to build it back up.
The youngest, a shovel raised above his head
like a sword, waves in the distance. The color
of fire.

Arboretum

Maybe the great tragedy of my childhood is that I could never keep a fish
alive for longer than a week. On Sunday, I'd slide a blade on the cheek
of a bag & watch everything empty into a round, glass bowl: water, fish, &
beige strands that rose when each suddenness rippled from its body.

By Thursday, the fish would stay still longer than usual, & by Saturday,
the inevitable. It happened many times. Gold ones with flecks of maroon
in the shape of Virginia would disappear behind the film of their eyes,
& the silver & black ones, they became a night full of stars.

In college, I watched a performance of *Romeo & Juliet* in the clearing
of an arboretum. I had brought someone with me. She
knew nothing about the fish. We were just starting to date,
though as I listened to the play, I knew we would never die together.

Sometimes the lessons are this quiet—someone whispering
as if feigning to be sincere. Afterwards, a few of the actors disappeared
into the woods, & we followed them to the edge, to a large, man-made pond
where a bridge spanned its width. We stood in the middle, tapping

the blond planks, their edges slightly green, fresh, & watched as the koi rose,
every color suddenly appearing to feed on our shadows.

The Metaphor of Sunlight Can Be Carried in a Bucket

As children, we waited for low tide & walked through
the slick thickness, threatening each step deeper than the next

in pools formed by the creek's edge. Schools of minnows
flashed in a stir of light. A half mile into the heart

of the canal, where it opens onto small islands of clumped cord
grass, we carried our buckets filled with fish. Slivers of silver

we returned to open space, spreading sunlight on water.

A Shadow of Gulls

Against the ferry's hull, a knot of water fell
when the engines died, & we drifted
between pilings woven together with rope.

As the boat pressed into boards, the crew appeared,
pulling free blocks chocked behind tires.

We drove over the cast-iron ramp that lay on the deck
                                        like a tongue

into the whiteness of the barrier island: a squat light-
house in the center of the neighborhood, the occasional white-
caps disappearing in the marina while intimacy lies
somewhere in the expanse of the salt marsh, life-
                        forms huddled in the mud.

Driving over the first of several small bridges,
creeks with words like *molasses* in their names,
I pointed over to the rasp of cord grass & told you how,

one summer, my brothers & I had seined the water
for young blue claws. Shiny, they reflected the sky
as we held each tender body, until they slid from our hands
& formed clouds in the green water.

That was years ago, & those crabs are either dead or
somewhere deep in the Atlantic, scavenging
the last piece of flesh on bone.

Maybe the skeleton of a whale, or maybe
even a man, whose last breath was not a scream,
but a few words, his name trapped in water,

                        ascending into light.

The Muse, *or* Stars Out on Interstate 81 South

On the tip of a hill, the silhouette is of something not of this world,
the body silent in the birth of another shadow, swelling still

among stars & veins. The sun dropping below the mountains left
hardly any light, except what glimmers on the membrane & slips

into the high grass. Alone, I pulled over to the side
of 81 where semis' blowing horns descend

beyond the sloped field. Pieces of barbed wire snapped from the line.
I stepped through the fence, its blood-colored rust rubbed into my hands.

For a moment, it is something that stays with me, like a memory
that does not give up easily. I try wiping my hands onto my jeans,

                                                                but nothing.

It is anything it wants to be—calf, half-life, angel—its fur a glaze
of cricket sounds & cool air, a thing of stars burnt into hooves, a haze,

& I stood there, not knowing whether it would be right to touch the one
not breathing, its nose drying in the grass next to my hands, grit

in the creases & burning now with the dust of splinters. Like flies,
my fingers hover over the dead face.

Willoughby Spit

In the middle of the tunnel, his car loses power & coasts,
but there is not enough momentum to push him through

the upswing. He stops, listens as horns begin to mimic
the beat of his hazards, drivers cursing behind the glass

are fishlike in the flashing light. *What,* he says, throwing his hands
in the air. There is no need to explain. Someone flips him off,

he does the same. When the wrecker arrives, traffic is backed up
past Willoughby Spit where, in this early morning, the thin boats tied

to the docks hint at some freedom for those stalled on the bridge.
The silhouette of the fleet across the bay starts to move,

maybe en route to somewhere faraway, where life is
inconvenienced by more than this. Cars in front, their lights

disappear inside themselves, inch forward as they prepare
to descend into the mouth of the tunnel, where there is some hope

of leaving it all behind.

2

Door That Always Opens

I would hear that one intended lonely sound,

the signature of the day, the ratchet of time

taking me a step toward here, now, and this

look back through the door that always closes.

—*William Stafford*

Between Rounds

Outside, barking dogs from our neighbor's yard
remind me of boxing matches my father & I
used to watch at the Amphib Base in Norfolk.

Enlisted men would punch each other,
round for round, until the sound of bells
smacked inside their minds.

She would not have recognized me then,
hiding behind my arms & laughing only
when they *didn't* fall.

One boxer barked whenever he punched.

I think about the way he fell to his knees
after he knocked his man out. Light
draped over raised gloves, & shadows

in his face shifted as he prayed, I thought,
to be understood. Now I know it was
something else, the way we smile
while musing on our survival.

The rest of the night, the crowd faked
jabs at ribs & lips while blows split
the bodies of those sprawled
on the smudged canvas.

I pull back the sheet & kiss her neck.

Because she has turned away from me,
she doesn't move. She doesn't say a word

when I reach into her hair, touching
until we both laugh.

One summer, I stacked wet bags of ice
onto conveyor belts lined with men,

some who had worked third shift through the night
while their wives, for the most part, slept alone.

I remember wearing gloves the first week
until the cloth rubbed the skin off my hands.

You'll lose the feeling in your fingers, they said.

I think about these men who didn't wear gloves.
One kept the name Korzeniowski tattooed on his hand.

A relative of Joseph Conrad's, he lived with two dancers
who wrapped themselves in sheets whenever he'd come

home from work. He told me how his name pressed
against their mouths, how he'd never read *Heart of Darkness*,
                              but that he had one.

I picture your feet bleeding
the way you said they bled

when your father, whose name I share,
picks you up, pulls you into the jungle,

away from Japanese soldiers
who had invaded the village

tearing through homes for Filipinas.
There are so many things that separate us.

I've tried identifying the obvious ones:
Language, anger, ourselves.

Even the uncles I never met:
Celso, who died in a death march,

Ted, with his children in the Islands,
or Manny, living in Oakland,

each voice, one I've never heard.
When I touch you, I touch years of silence.

You must know this: I feel pathetic
pressing rewind on the tape player,

listening again to a strange voice
repeat "Amá" or "Tatay" for *Father*.

I couldn't cry or you would yell
Putang ina, your anger always untranslatable.

Christmases when you were *out at sea,*
we'd gather around a tape recorder,

so you would hear your children singing;
only, I could never finish a song.

I'd picture your face listening
to my voice break, & it made me stop.

Postcards from Spain or Italy,
with our names printed in your thin, neat hand,

would arrive just days before Christmas Eve;
always the description of chapels you had visited.

Always an attempt at redemption.
Years ago I found one of those postcards

clumped in the coat pocket of a suit
I'd worn as a child. I must have taken it with me

to Midnight Mass, folded it during the offerings
until it fit the size of my small hands.

The other night, I told a story about waking,
how I walked through the house one morning
when I was young &, from the kitchen window,
watched as you buried my dog.

You stood over the hole, next to a pile
of dirt & clay. The shovel shook in your hands,
& for some reason, I forgot to mention this part,

the most important part,

that you, *Tatay,* were the one crying.

We share the burden of another language,
each punch-drunk syllable or swiftly-thrown vowel.

Do you hear yourself in my voice,
pounding into recognition?

Hindî ako mabuting magsalitâ ng inyong wikà
means *I don't speak your language very well.*

This is not what I want to say.

After the boxers left the ring, & the crowd
rose from their seats & shouted, the lights
beating down into figures of smoke,
your hand lifted mine above my head
as if I had or maybe we had won
something together, survived another night
in the long history of fathers & sons.

Maybe we were only between rounds
ourselves, resting for the years ahead,
but it felt right to be with you in that den
filled with failure & victory & the roar
settling back into shadows, after all
the fights have been forgotten.

Memory in the Shape of a House Made of Doors

If anything, it is like the house his friend had told him about
made completely out of doors, somewhere in Colorado

or California. He liked the idea: A house built with nothing
but used doors, each with its own history of useless hinges

& rusty locks. In a busy deli in Chapel Hill, he listened
to a friend describe how each wall was a wall of doors pieced

together. Workers behind the counter were yelling customers' names.
As he sat there listening, he thought of his sister, years ago, in bed

after the car accident had left her paralyzed & unable to speak.
If the door to her room was closed, he would check on her.

He took this moment & slowly pushed it open,
walked inside to find her still there, waiting for anyone.

When she saw it was him, she wanted to say his name.
She tried, but the word became only a breath in the room

where the walls were like the walls in his friend's story—
his memory, a house made of nothing

but doors. He heard his name in someone else's mouth,
saw it was only a girl behind the counter calling

across a room filled with bodies coming & going.

Shelter

Have you forgotten the way my face winced at my father
when, instead of shaking your hand, he walked off sputtering
mestizo in a language I knew you didn't understand?
I have closed a small space of my heart, packed it
with jars of figs, canned tomatoes, blankets, & jugs
of fresh water. We could open them, dip our fingers
first into the preserves & then into each other's mouth.
Inside these walls, under blankets, we could wait
for the storm.

Black Sea Bass

It lay in a cooler filled with ice
the night we were out of power
from the storm. Its skin was gray
when I reached inside, not the way
I first pulled it from the ocean.
Sharp yellow tips of fins stretched
as it raised to where my brother & I
leaned over the side of a head boat.

We were talking about the future.
Our other brother was suffering
a hangover somewhere in Blacksburg
after a week of engineering classes.
But we weren't him, & we didn't know
what it was he really wanted, though
for whatever reason, I wish he could
have been with us as fish appeared
out of nowhere. The storm came through
the night & ran a finger along the city's
power lines, as if playing guitar. Primaries
snapped loose & danced on sidewalks
while the music of fire pounded onto roofs.

That morning I went into the backyard, spread
a paper covering stories of the storm,
smeared scales with a blade and gutted the fish,
peeling its hard stomach out. There,
as I slit it open, I found three baby crabs
it must have swallowed whole, still filled
with blue & green bending on their claws.
It reminded me of a time my brothers & I had spent
on Ocracoke, when we waded in parts of the salt marsh
where young blue claws darted out from clouds in the water,
their bodies disappearing into the clear, inevitable distance.

Birthmark

After they make love, he slides down so his face rests near her waist. The light by the bed casts its nets that turn into shadows. They both fall asleep. When he wakes, he finds a small patch of birthmarks on her thigh, runs his finger over each island, a speck of light brown bundled with others to form an archipelago on her skin. For him, whose father is from the Philippines, it is the place he has never been, filled with hillsides of rice & fish, different dialects, a family he wants to touch, though something about it all is untouchable, like love, balanced between desire & longing, the way he reaches for her now, his hand pressed near this place that seems so foreign, so much a part of him that for a moment, he cannot help it, he feels whole.

3

Inevitable Distance

But none would sleep,

none wanted to be a river,

none loved the great leaves,

none, the blue tongue of the beach

—*Federico García Lorca*

Miscarriage

We'd been trying for months
when, one night, we heard
what sounded like a baby,
its cries sharpening outside.
Our neighbors had gathered
in the backyard & stared
high into one of the trees
where a young raccoon clung
to a branch bending slowly.
There were holes in the trunk
where its mother had nested,
& this one, no bigger than
your hand, it seemed, flashed
its eyes in fear when spotlight
ricocheted through leaves.
I think about this animal's
face, how it was taken away
from the tree boarded up
now, its mother long gone.
I take comfort in forgetting
the details & hold our son.

Five about Flowers

One summer I could not walk into one of the rooms where we lived without first seeing them spread about, watered, in handfuls. Daisies.

Remember this story about the couple, when they were dating
he had given her flowers, & she hid them in a book, let them dry

in between the pages. Petals became paper & the paper petals.

The bulbs you can break apart like loaves of bread, the damp husk smell that

                                                                          stays

on your skin for days until one night, there is no washing it away, you wake

from it lingering on her lips. Pink flowers, petals caught in a sway.

They want you to think that the fireworks, brilliant streaks of green & pink, are like flowers in the night sky, but the ash rains down on the crowd.

The papery blackness, pieces of the dome no one has ever seen, burns.

In the papery white smoke stretching like a wing from the side of the train.
This wing spreads across the platform & joins with others waiting to leave.

Some hang out of windows & try to reach those below—*There now,*
someone says & lifts up roses, knocking against the cold glass.

Trying to get your attention.

Corolla

A man edges his way toward a herd of horses
that have slowed in the receding water.

He offers one a handful of vegetables while
his other hand comes into view like a bird from far off, hovering
just so above the horse & its mane.

Distance closes between his fingertips & its eyes. Like flames,
thin chest-high waves finish into the sand, the same sand
where we built a bonfire the night before,

where the ashes lifted in their own small whirl,
                                  burning out over the beach.

He reminds me of an artist examining a block of wood
until the figure descends upon him, the way light falls naturally.

I met a man who used to carve saints,
                              large Bartholomews hunched
from the weight of their skins & Agneses who seemed to wince
at the thought of dead lambs in their own arms.

Their faces were bloody, & still, he kept going.

It's the same, standing here instead of stepping through the sea-
oats & sandspurs lifted lightly by the wind
to hold the artist in this moment,

as he feeds something wild, as he loses it all to time
& watches the herd storm into water.

Hunger

The morning after their son is born, he goes home to feed the cats.
He drives through Ghent, with its thick Victorians, & crosses the tracks

to the edge of Riverview where the same-styled homes stand,
though the paint peeling from each shutter makes them seem ruined

somehow. At the stoplight, he watches a transvestite slowly cross the street.
Her body hunched, protective, she is nursing a cup of coffee, & the steam

that rises now, the soul of it, its warmth vanishes in front of her face.
He thinks of their son, newborn, sealing his lips to his mother's breast,

& it is this thought that he carries across the Lafayette Bridge, the cold
water stirring underneath. At home, the cats lick their bowls clean.

A Few Words on Rome, *or* The Neighbor Who Never Waves

Passing Viareggio, he sees his reflection in the window
& past that, part of a beach where it is said the poet's

body washed on shore, where a pyre was built there
on the sand, the blaze filling him until his chest burst

& Byron reached in to grab the heart. Who cares
if it never happened? This story of madness never hurt

anyone, not even Shelley, who would have loved
what they have done to him. His heart in Rome. His body,

                                        the wind.

Passing Viareggio, he notices the beach just as the old woman
sitting across from him whispers, *beautiful eyes,* in Italian.

She is talking to him, the one thinking about Shelley's death,
& he looks at her. *Cosa?* he says. She is seventy. She says

she is happy to be traveling. Her daughter lives in Rome.
It is Christmas Eve. He tries to keep up in the conversation,

though he doesn't understand half of the words; it makes her happy
to see him nod at the right moments. Then he understands & then
doesn't.

It goes on this way for some time.

Years later, he finds himself driving home through Norfolk.
He passes a park where a boy's body was found the day before.

A victim of a drive-by. There are flowers left under one
of the trees. It is early evening, & the streets nearby are beginning

to fill with bodies. His wife leans over to him & kisses his chin
without saying a word.

It seems things happen in life for no reason at all.

Turning onto their street, they see the neighbor who never waves back.

Viareggio is gone. He remembers it only for the story of the body
& for the words *beautiful eyes.* No one has ever told him that before.

He blushes. She asks where he is from. He says America. He mentions
his father is from the Philippines. She claps her hands. She must tell him how

industrious she thinks Filipinos are. She tells him
they are the best maids she has ever had.

Maybe the neighbor doesn't really care. Maybe the neighbor is so
engrossed in his pile of leaves & garbage that he has not formed

an opinion on their marriage. He hasn't considered the young couple
across the street. The husband who is *mixed* like his dog, the one

with a brown & a blue eye. The one he scolds for shitting in the house.

The old woman reached in a bag & pulled out a fiasco of wine
& clementine oranges. They peeled them together & drank

until they reached the first station in Rome. Here she gathered her things
& kissed him on the cheek. He was taking the train into the heart

of the city, where he would join the crowd in front of St. Peter's
who were singing in different languages, some singing off-key.

Weight

On the steps of Santa Croce, a woman held her child,
his hand cupped above a plate of coins.

Nevermind them,

a guide said to the group of tourists swarming around him.
Gypsies drug their kids to look like that.

The boy's eyes gazed into the roof of his skull.

His jaw fell & struggled to close,

mouthing a language he had found written on the walls of blood.

The pietà is inside, the guide said as they filed, one by one,

into darkness,

over a roomful of bodies.

Bonfire

We build a bonfire in the backyard.
The world is a different place now,
someone says, & they are the first
to light a match & let it set it off.
Light hammers the surrounding dark
each time fire strikes a rusty nail
hidden somewhere in there. We
widen our circle away from it once
its core fills, then with the night
cooling off everything, we draw
ourselves in so that we can have
a chance to see the embers gray,
their tiny hearts pounding away.

Night Feeding

Our son cries from the other room,
& it is this sound that wakes me,
                              wakes us both.

Because we share in caring for him, I ask,
                    Isn't it your turn?

His voice, new, loosens another foot of string,
a kite floating in the night sky.

So serious, you whisper,
              Just give me another second,

then lay your head back.

I find him sitting up, his hands gripping the crib,
his voice suddenly gone when

I pull him to my chest, & we return
to you, asleep, your breasts full
                         of dreams.

4

Undoing

I don't want to scare you;

after death there are two alternatives,

both heartless:

memory & forgetfulness

—*Jon Anderson*

Living Together

Bruce Denbigh placed a stick in
the spokes of my tire, & I went flying,
just for a second, over the pavement.
In the shower, he lifts his chin & tells her
the story behind this scar. She parts her hair
to show him where a rock had cut into her scalp.
I was so young, she says, laughing,
I only remember walking home, dazed,
& for a moment, water gathers in the cusp
of his palm when he traces it with a finger,
then touches her lips. *What about this?* she asks,
placing her nail over the crescent moon-
shape resting on his shoulder.
My sister, he says. He doesn't explain
she has been dead for almost half of his life.
There is no need, yet as they dry off, he has an impulse
to mention this scar has outlived the memory
of her voice. *We fought about something,*
but I don't remember what.
She rubs her towel over his shoulder, the way
his sister tapped a cloth lightly over the gelled gash,
sending a message over all of his screaming
to find him here, years later, listening for the first time
to the way she tried to comfort him without words.

In Strange Circles

How is it that, years later, after watching a few men along Franklin heave bloated bags of trash into the back of a truck, I remember that summer at Atlantic Beach when hundreds of man-of-wars had washed onto the shore, & though a voice on the radio kept warning everyone to "stay away from the oceanfront," we drove there anyway, just to see our blurred reflections in the steamy globes slowly deflating in the sun? Later that night, underneath the pier the sounds & lights from the bars along the boardwalk receded into the on-shore break, this world slipped into other worlds. We touched by accident as we felt over the sand, patting down shells so that we'd have a place to lie back, maybe view the light leaking in between boards. She said, "Don't even think about it," & we laughed as she threw her bra into the water, the padded cups floating on a sheet that would eventually cover us.

Translation

We thought nothing of it, he says,
though some came so close to where we slept.

I try to see him as a boy,
back in the Philippines, waking

to the sound of machine guns.
His family would spend their morning

spreading a paste over the sores
of the house's thick walls.

He tells how he touched
points where bullets entered,

his *fingers,* he says, *disappeared into the holes,*

as if inside there existed a space
where everything from this world could vanish.

Here we could place the memory of my sister,
his daughter, who died after a car wreck.

Wedge her into the smoky path
                            & cover her in sunlight.

The family next door is raking leaves in the yard.

A father scolds his children for jumping
into large piles he arranged into a crescent moon.

We cannot hear them from inside,
but I feel they are frightened as he grabs both of them
                            around the waist & spins.

I wait for the ending to my father's story,
but he is too busy smiling, as if enjoying the silence

of bullets frozen there in his mind.

In the Romance of Grief

There are three oaks in the yard.

As saplings, their translucent
branches were braided, evening

after evening, so they might grow
together, woven with years.

Inside the house, two girls & a boy wait
for their father to come to the table set

with bowls of steamy rice,
                    collards & pansit.

He walks into the house & washes
his hands in the kitchen sink, touching

his wife's hands with his damp fingers
as she passes behind him. They laugh,

& later, this simple gesture of love
will be forgotten, like many others before it.

Perhaps this world survives its losses
through its forgetting.

In the romance of grief,
the boy at the table stops singing

because his father silences him
with a look. They fold their hands,

bless this moment. Outside,
the leaves on the branches

look like little hands patting
the bark of white oak.

His work unfolds in the darkness.
The next evening, he must begin

again, weaving branches together.

Everything is considered holy.

A portrait hanging in the corner of a room.

Boxes of old clothes, all sizes of the body

that grew & then disappeared. Its pants
& shirts, relics. Its scent of dust & mildew.

Even the white oaks are holy in their undoing
as the trunks fan away again into three

separate trees, the wind weaving between
the branches, the ghost of work.

Does it matter that the portrait looks nothing
like the girl? Does it matter that the mother

has let the clothes remain in boxes
among other boxes in a room of the house?

In the romance of grief, there are rooms that remain
closed, & for this, the house closes in on the living.

What of the light outside? What of the bird lighting
on the green clothesline near the shirts & pants?

One summer, the mother walked out into the backyard
& hung damp clothes on the line.

A deer appeared at the edge of the yard & then slowly
walked toward her. The doe was nervous, its breathing

moving quickly underneath its coat of fur, & the mother
did not move as the animal approached the line

& licked the cool water dripping from one of the shirts.

And happiness?

             Let us say it was the moment
she came back into the house & forgot
that it ever happened at all. It was months
until she remembered again. Her son had called
& she told him the story as if it was all just
nothing.

And sadness?

             Of course. It could be anything.
The season of drought. The doe so thirsty
it was unafraid of the woman taking pins
& pinching the wet cloth to the thin line
so that it would hold in the wind. Anything.
Or even the coffee she made with spoonfuls of sugar
& cream. She sat at the table, alone, & stared
at the molded tin picture of *La Ultima Cena*,
The Last Supper, hanging on the wall.
When she looked down at her cup,
the cream had settled to the bottom
& left only traces of itself on the surface.

And the world now?

             It comes & goes
as it pleases. The wind through trees.
A doe walking back into the woods.
The settling of dust on the glass
covering a portrait, or in the grooves
of metal where all the faces are
of someone—apostles, savior,
betrayer.

This Poetry

It is where she has gone. A spoon clicks
in her mouth while her eyes fall back,

& the one holding her hand is not me
or you. It is a boy, her brother, & he is afraid,

though he remembers something about pressing
a spoon to her tongue so that metal catches

the flesh, so that the tongue does not follow
the eyes into leaving a part of this world.

Years later, this boy will read he was wrong
for using a spoon. He will spend the summer

lifeguarding at a pool, & more than once, he will
hold a body while it seizes in waist-high water.

Each one returns the same way, a pause & then
their life, all they have ever known, rushing back

into the mind. Forget the boy in the beginning.
He has grown into someone who spends too much

time remembering. For this, he has already lost a part
of himself, & from those people he saved, holding

them in the sun as they came to, the color in their eyes
sharp as glass, there was a time when he thought

this could be her, a body becoming weightless.
Then a stranger cried in his arms. She didn't

know anyone around her, especially him.
It did not matter. This is not about remembering.

Forget there was ever a spoon. Forget the sound
metal makes against the teeth & the tongue.

Forget it all & come back to your life.

Other Books in the Crab Orchard Award Series in Poetry

Muse
Susan Aizenberg

This Country of Mothers
Julianna Baggott

White Summer
Joelle Biele

In Search of the Great Dead
Richard Cecil

Consolation Miracle
Chad Davidson

Names above Houses
Oliver de la Paz

The Star-Spangled Banner
Denise Duhamel

Pelican Tracks
Elton Glaser

Winter Amnesties
Elton Glaser

Fabulae
Joy Katz

Train to Agra
Vandana Khanna

Crossroads and Unholy Water
Marilene Phipps

Year of the Snake
Lee Ann Roripaugh

Misery Prefigured
J. Allyn Rosser

Becoming Ebony
Patricia Jabbeh Wesley